KEEP BREATHING

a book of micro-poems

Other Books by Ann Christine Tabaka

4,500 Miles as the Falcon Flies
Finding my family

Overcast Mind
My life in poems

It Is Still Morning
A Continuation of my Life in Poems

When Dragons and Angels Collide
Modern & Traditional Haiku & Senryu

Everlasting
A Lifetime of Poems

The Sound of Dragonfly Wings
Haiku & Senryu

Reaching for Dawn
Poems

Just Breathe
Micro-poems

No More Hallelujahs
Poetry chapbook

Words Spill Out
Poems

Website: https://annchristinetabaka.com

KEEP BREATHING

a book of micro-poems

Ann Christine Tabaka

Keep Breathing Copyright © 2020: Ann Christine Tabaka. All rights reserved. No part of this book may be used or reproduced in any manner whatsoever without written permission except in the case of reprints in the context of reviews. This Collection is protected under U.S. and International Copyright laws.

Interior design by

CTU
Publishing Group

a division of *Creative Talents Unleashed*

www.creativetalentsunleashed.com

1st Edition
Printed in the United States of America
ISBN: 9798611875094

Cover Design: Raja Williams
Photograph Credits: Cat Eyes; Dragon; and Teardrop
Images from: Pixabay.com
All other photographs taken by Ann Christine Tabaka©

Dedication

I dedicate this book to my mother,
Antoinette Mary Tabaka (R.I.P.),
who taught me to believe in myself
and to never give up.

Prologue

Keep Breathing is my second book of micro-poems, and my tenth book of poetry, which includes two Haiku & Senryu books. As I mentioned in *Just Breathe*, my first book of micro-poems, I love the challenge of telling a complete story in as few words as possible – like a breath of fresh air. It allows the reader's imagination to fill in the details and paint its own picture.

CHAPTERS

One - ***Climbing***

Two - ***Just for Fun***

Three - ***Soaring***

Four - ***Falling***

Five - ***Living***

CLIMBING

I stand
I fall
I run
I crawl
I stand again
I walk to win

- determination

I walked inside
your love
like a child
into a candy store

Seed Heads

©*Ann Christine Tabaka*

once again
autumn burst upon the scene
scattering dried seeds
in its path

- rebirth

trying to put life's pieces together
one brick at a time

- rebuilding

morning opens her curtains
to the song of birds

- daybreak

hiding in the shadow of winter
spring is just a wish away

– new birth

I am sober now
I gave you up
a long time ago

I remember
you walked into my life
and left with my heart
it takes great effort
to grow a new life

the righteous man
stands before himself
and no one else
none other shall speak for him
nor carry his burden

seeds of hope
scattered on a whisper

                              - *prayers*

JUST FOR FUN

the sentence is so long,
I cannot catch my breath,
so commas are my friend,
until I reach the end

oh fiddle sticks
and pumpkin seeds
here we go again
you think that I
would figure it out
at least now and then

a hole in one sock
a lonely mate
the mismatched pile
hoping for new life

romping through the house
kittens chasing imaginary prey

- playtime

stealing noses
tickling toesies
grandpas are such great fun

if I hang upside-down
from this tree
long enough
I shall become
a child again

Pixabay.com

playing hide and seek
bright eyes smile back
through black fur
the purr is a dead giveaway

night owl
on the prowl
seeking prey
at end of day
as darkness falls
her instinct calls

SOARING

a time before time
reaches out
and grabs us
by the imagination

hope is a song
sung softly in the night
whispered on a prayer

Fuchsia

©*Ann Christine Tabaka*

red flowers hang
from a basket of desire
luring winged jewels

- hummingbirds

autumn dresses in orange and gold
while winter wears her coat of white
spring paints the world green
but summer's vibrant song
creates a multicolor dream

sun streaming through
a stained glass wish
bestowing promises of joy

I walked away from somewhere safe
stood on the edge of risk
stepped off into the unknown
and flew into the future

journeys of the imagination
bring a joy that cannot be matched

– reading books

Lewes, Delaware

©*Ann Christine Tabaka*

rainy morning
on the beach
a water world
plays on the imagination
soaring above the clouds
I find myself

it was delicious from the start
there was not any part
that did not satisfy

> *- the experience*

what you feel in your heart
what you know in your mind
is integrated into the whole
it is the universe that is you

loving you
is the hardest thing
I have ever done

- sacrifice

whispers in the dark
all that is left of our love
reaching out for you
you are no longer there

– empty nights

the empty space within me
is the place you used to fill

beauty
overtaken by pain
hobbles along a desperate edge
between life and death

once again I climb too high
and once again I fall
a lesson someday I must learn
at the cost of all

I do not have
the energy
to fight anymore
for the battle is within

you reached out your hand for me
only to withdraw it
seeking youth
when winter came

a cold wind wraps
me in its clutches
strangling the breath
from my lungs

– winter gale

we tried too hard
fire and ice
we repelled each other

I am beginning to think
that none of this is worth it

– the struggle

sadness of an eternity
caught between
the pages of my life

- my story

the price of sin
is not death
it is having to
live with oneself

sometimes silence
is not golden
when there is nothing
left to say

- emptiness

in the void
there are no days
nor nights
only long stretches
of being

- sleeplessness

it was a long time ago
the pain is gone
but scars remain

- divorce

reaching for infinity
we speed past
the star we seek

- ambition

allow yourself
to fall apart
and
come back together
when you are ready

– grieving

the taste of sweetness on my tongue
has now turned sour

– lost love

had I known then
what I know now
my life would be
a different place

counting on false hope
leads to despair

> *– impossible dreams*

Pixabay.com

ancient maps warned us
but only told half truths
we are beyond the edge
and dragons are not the threat

– the danger is us

LIVING

we strive for perfection
only to fail
while ignoring
the attainable goal
within our reach

oh elusive sleep
you evade my every grasp
as the small hours creep by

– insomnia

Buster

©*Ann Christine Tabaka*

the boisterous rumbling of a kitten
all too soon becomes
the muted purr of old age

Pixabay.com

growing up
we did not speak of such things
we turned our heads
and hid our eyes

the innocence of childhood
washed away
with a single tear

sometimes words are not enough
but words are all we have

- *sympathy*

sorry ...

a word that says so much
yet says nothing
escapes easily from the lips
but not always from the heart

– apologies

I have been shaken
mistaken and forsaken
I no longer know the way

time is repeating
retreating and depleting
until there is none left

sometimes things rhyme
not because it was planned
but because the words just fit
into the flow of thought
and sometimes we need to let be
what is meant to be

ignorance shouts
its demands
while wisdom speaks
with a dulcet voice

each teardrop
holds a story of
its own pain or joy

time stands still for no man
it swiftly passes by
the moments years and ages
as if on wings they fly
so catch and keep each second
and never let it die
and never question why

searching to find myself
you are my way back home

                                                - *illumination*

Knocking

©*Ann Christine Tabaka*

I thought I was so clever
'til truth knocked on my door

                           - *awakening*

Books on a Nightstand

©*Ann Christine Tabaka*

books piled high
on a nightstand
waiting to be read

- sleep beckons

a thin line of hope
separates us from the damned

– whispered prayers

when it doesn't matter anymore
all pain and anxiety will evaporate

– letting go

floating on a cloud
of indecision
high above the
pinnacle of reason

- stalemate

I have no reason to complain
I am who I was meant to be

- destiny

never think that you are too big
to give the little guy a break
you never know when you may be
the one who needs a hand up

we all make mistakes
and sometimes they are irreversible
so we just have to learn to live with them

                                        - *responsibility*

Your Shadow

© Ann Christine Tabaka

you were always
the only one
even now that
you are gone
your shadow
still follows me

wisdom speaks
with open eyes
and a trusting heart
it is not always
the way of man
who wants to
close the door

sometimes clever words
just fall into place
other times the struggle
is riddled with anxiety

do not let regret
steal precious
minutes from you
you cannot hold tears
in your pocket

by the time we realize
that we cannot turn back
it is too late to
take control of the reins

inside the box we stifle and wilt
outside the box we grow
yet so many try to fit
within the crushing weight

what is left when everything is gone
only yourself
you cannot compete against the world
you will never win

May to September

©*Ann Christine Tabaka*

September comes too fast
while May lingers on the cusp

                     – changing seasons

I do not have to be right
I just do not want to be wrong
somewhere in between
I'll find the words to my song

- compromise

About the Poet

Ann Christine Tabaka has been nominated for the 2017 Pushcart Prize in Poetry. Her poems have received many awards and have been published in numerous national and international publications both online and in print.

Visit her website at
https://annchristinetabaka.com

Made in the USA
Monee, IL
08 August 2022